Wasting THE Wasters

DR. D. K. OLUKOYA

Warfare Prayer Series 18

Wasting the Wasters

DR. D. K. OLUKOYA

WASTING THE WASTERS
Published - July 2005 AD
Re-printed - 2011 AD

ISBN 978-0692258255

© 2005 The Battle Cry Christian Ministries

322, Herbert Macaulay Way,
Yaba P O Box 12272, Ikeja, Lagos
Website www.battlecryng.com
email, sales@battlecryng.com
Phone 2348033044239,01-8044415

I salute my wonderful wife, Pastor Shade, for her invaluable support in the ministry.

I appreciate her unquantifiable support in the book ministry as the cover designer, art editor and art adviser

All Scripture quotation is from the King James Version of the Bible

All rights reserved.
We prohibit reproduction in whole or part without written permission.

TABLE OF CONTENT

CHAPTER   PAGE

1. WASTING THE WASTERS......................................4

2. WICKEDNESS MUST DIE......................................20

3. BURIED BUT NOT DEAD.......................................36

CHAPTER ONE

WASTING THE WASTERS

The kingdom of darkness is filled with different kinds of powers. In spiritual warfare parlance, there are powers known as wasters. They destroy and waste precious lives as well as bright prospects. The power of the wasters makes so many people to miss out on God's marvelous and gracious plans.

How many potential geniuses have been reduced to wrecks by the wasters? Lots of stars which would have caused a global change have been destroyed by the operations and manipulations of the wasters. The time to dispossess the kingdom of darkness has come. The holy anger of God must rise within you. Enough is enough. You have to possess your possessions. You must determine within yourself not to be wasted.

I congratulate you, on having in your hands the nuggets that will empower you to waste the wasters. The Bible makes it clear that:

Isaiah 49:24-26: *Shall the prey be taken from the mighty, or the lawful captive delivered? But thus saith the LORD, Even the captives of the mighty shall be taken away, and the prey of the terrible shall be delivered: for I will contend with him that contendeth with thee, and I will save thy children. And I will feed them that oppress thee with their own flesh; and they shall be drunken with their own blood, as with sweet wine: and all flesh shall know that I the LORD am thy*

Saviour and thy Redeemer, the mighty One of Jacob.

The heavens must rumble and the earth must quake. Power must change hands. The time for your deliverance has come. Whatever power that wants to waste your life must be wasted by the everlasting arm and power of God. The strong man who has been holding you down, must hear the word of the Lord and let you go. The resurrection power of God, must raise you from the valley to the mountain top. Testimonies must fill your mouth because God has opened a book of remembrance concerning your own case.

NEVER TO BE WASTED

God did not create you to have a wasted life. God has a glorious and marvelous plan and purpose for your life. You are not on the face of the earth by mere chance or mistake. There is a divine purpose you need to fulfil.

Satan and all his cohorts are the brains behind wasting the lives of people and destroying the destinies of multitudes. When you allow sin and the operations of satan and his agents in your life, you are at the verge of experiencing a ruined life and destiny. However, when you discover and step into the divine plan and purpose for your life, you become immuned to the operations of the power of the waster.

WASTING THE WASTERS

It pains my heart greatly, to see myriads of people, day in, day out being rubbished by the power of the waster. The African continent had contributed in no small measure to the operations of the power of the waster. There are some people who have been praying ceaselessly without having a breakthrough because of the intricate ways the waster's powers operate. Unfortunately, many evil foundations are speaking woe, failure and calamity to the lives of some people. To remain in ignorance as to the operations of the power of the waster, is to die quickly! Ignorance is even more than a disease; it is a sure path to supporting the devil's desire to end your life. That is why the Bible says;

Isaiah 5:13-14: Therefore my people are gone into captivity, because they have no knowledge: and their honourable men are famished, and their multitude dried up with thirst. Therefore hell hath enlarged herself, and opened her mouth without measure: and their glory, and their multitude, and their pomp, and he that rejoiceth, shall descend into it.

The first step you must take, to get out of the cobweb of the power of the wasters, is to know that the operations are real. This revelation is not to instill fear into you, but rather to make you to be aware of the truth. It is the truth that will set you free.

My earnest plea and prayer to God is that, the

mighty hand of God will deliver you from the jaws of the power of the wasters in Jesus name. Then, you will be at liberty to enter into your divine destiny.

A WASTED LIFE!

Quite a number of people live wasted lives. This fact becomes clear when you pause and take a look at the people in your neighbourhood or in your nation. So many people only come to the face of the earth to eat, sleep, marry and die! They come to the face of the earth unnoticed and leave no footprint for posterity to see. Call upon the name of God and cry to your heavenly father by praying thus:

"I refuse to be wasted, in the name of Jesus".

Please give special and ample time to this prayer point How many neighbours, relatives, or friends of yours have come to the face of the earth and died without fulfilling the divine purpose? For you to breathe at this moment and also be able to read this book is a testimony. My prayer is that, you will locate the divine will of God for your life, so that before your time is up, you would have been able to cause a change which will outlive time and eternity.

THE POWER OF THE WASTER

The phenomenon of the power of the wasters is not a new invention. It had been from the creation of the world. It operated at the time of the children of Israel. The power of the wasters disguised as the old serpent, showed up in the garden of Eden and polluted it. Right from that time, the whole of human race have been plunged into misery and gloom.

The fall of man in the garden of Eden, is what is responsible for the mysterious occurrences that have bedeviled humanity till now. Your decision, will go a long way to determine your future and that of generations yet unborn. You will agree with me that the decision that Adam and Eve took which made them to disobey God by eating the forbidden fruit has continued to affect everybody on the face of the earth. Human depravity, is entrenched into the lives of everybody who comes to the face of the earth. Therefore, be careful on the decision you take because the repercussion might be unbearable not only to you but unto up and coming generations.

The children of Israel did not learn their lessons. They vacillated between serving God and serving satan. They lived an up and down life and this made the anger of God to burn over them. God told them:

Number 14:32-33: *But as for you, your carcases, they shall fall in this wilderness. And your children shall wander in the wilderness forty years, and bear your whoredoms, until your carcases be wasted in the wilderness*

Disobedience to the word of God, will bring the anger and wrath of God over your life. An unstable life will be opened to all manners of satanic assault. Living on the mountain today and valley tomorrow will expose you to the arrows of the enemies. That is why you must make up your mind to lead a life that will be pleasing to God. This is what will build a wall of fire round you and will make you to be free from the operations of the power of the wasters.

THE WILDERNESS EXPERIENCE

There might be a time in your life, when you may have to pass through the wilderness experience. The wilderness experience will either make or mar you. You are either going to be wasted or watered to flourish after passing through the wilderness experience. For the children of Israel, so many of them were wasted after passing through the wilderness experience. Only Joshua and Caleb refused to be wasted.

Our Lord and Saviour Jesus Christ had to pass through the wilderness experience, as a preparation for the herculean ministry of rescuing humanity from the burden of sin. During the wilderness experience, he had three testing temptations. If he had fallen into temptation, he would not have been able to have a fulfilled ministry. The victory over the wilderness experience resulted into the victory which he had throughout his earthly ministry. Therefore, after going through temptations, you will either become better in life and ministry or you will become battered.

Beloved, the trials of your faith, the temptations you are passing through and the ordeals you are facing might be a test, or your own wilderness experience. The purpose of God is that, you should not be destroyed by trials. You are expected to experience fulfillment, after going through trials. The plan of God for you is that testimonies of triumph should fill your mouth. The hand and power of God will see you through the wilderness experience of life. Know that you are not alone. As a child of God, the presence of God is with you as you are passing through the wilderness experience of life. Victory over the turbulence and torrents of life will be yours as you put your hope, trust and faith in God.

The Bible says;

Proverb 3:5-6: *Trust in the LORD with all thine heart; and lean not unto thine own understanding. In all thy ways acknowledge him, and he shall direct thy paths*

During the wilderness experience of life, look up to God. Get involved with studying the word of God, so as to know the mind of God. Pray without ceasing. Tell God to hold your hands, so that you will not fall into the hands of the wasters. God will make you not to fall during the wilderness experience. He will empower you to fire on and forge ahead until you become what God wants you to be.

DIVINE SECURITY

The activities of the wasters are evident in our days. However, there is a promise of divine security for those in Christ Jesus. It is divine security, that will make you to be immune to satanic arrows. Nothing whatsoever will shake or trouble a child of God who is divinely secured. This is as a result of the fact that you will become the apple of God's eye and no one can attempt to tamper or touch the apple of God's eye. Not even satan can attempt it, let alone his agents.

Psalm 91:5-6: Thou shalt not be afraid for the terror by night; nor for the arrow that flieth by day; Nor for the pestilence that walketh in darkness; nor for the destruction that wasteth at noonday.

It is saddening, that great stars are being cut off at the prime of their lives. Thus, when the Bible talks about the destruction that wasteth at noonday you should realise that the Bible is making us to discover a number of young stars whom the devil and agents of darkness have wasted during their teenage years. That is why I pity people who are postponing the day of their salvation. Little do they know that, they might be wasted by the wasters before tomorrow comes. Let me make it categorically clear to you, life without Christ will become crooked and it will result into shattered dreams.

How dull human beings could be? What will it take for you to take a step of faith and get saved? Why must people just allow their lives to be wasted without having Christ? It will not take you a whole day for you to give your life to Christ and start afresh with God.

There is no enjoyment your can derive from the pleasures of sin for a moment, which can be commensurate with the consequences of sins here on earth and throughout eternity. Sin will give an express permission to wasters to destroy your life.

IT IS REAL

The spirit of the wasters is rest. What is the meaning of the word waste? To waste means to damage and destroy something gradually. To waste is to spend something carelessly or without thought. To waste also means to use something ineffectively. Rendering something or somebody worthless, useless and impotent. It also connotes wasting a particular thing or a person. To be wasted is to lose strength, vigour, and vitality. To waste, is to make a strong man, woman or team become feeble. To waste, is to take an advantage of something in a negative way. To waste, is to fail to use something profitably. When you allow something or somebody to lie unused, unproductive and valueless, you are wasting it.

Apart from that, to waste, is to cause something or a particular situation to get worse or decay. It means, causing something to fade away, misapplying somebody or something, misusing the particular thing and thereby spoiling the thing.

Therefore the power of the wasters is not what you should joke with. You are to cry unto God so that you will not end up as a casualty in the hands of the wasters. You must also render all the plans and activities of the enemies impotent so that the wasters will not have any access to your life.

AREAS OF OPERATIONS OF THE WASTERS

Having understood what is known as the wasters, it is pertinent for me to show you the areas or things that the wasters could waste. The operations of the wasters can be carried out in the following areas:
1. Opportunities
2. Money.
3. Resources
4. Time
5. Blessings
6. Virtues

7. Talents
8. Career
9. Calling
10. Marriage
11. Virginity
12. Anointing
13. Labour
14. Health
15. Knowledge
16. Children
17. Birthright
18. Parents
19. Friends
20. Life
21. Destiny

A CASE STUDY

The children of Israel still remains an important case study in the area of the operations of the wasters. The wasters not only prolonged their journey to the Canaan land but also wasted their lives. They were at the edge of the promised land but could not enter. For about 38 years, they were going about a place called Kadesh Barnea. About three million people were going in circles for almost thirty eight years because the wasters came in. They were wasted because they listened to powers that divert destinies.

If you have discovered that you have been roaming about the market square of life, you must pray to get rid of the waster's power. If you also notice that there has been repeated failures in your life, you must pray against the power of the wasters.

THE MANIFESTATIONS OF THE WASTER'S SPIRIT

When the vagabond life is in place, progress in life will become elusive. In other words, you may not be able to point to a tangible thing that you have achieved, you may be moving but progress might not be achievable. This is what the waster spirit can do in the life of a man.

The undertone of the spirit of the waster might be responsible, when you are dreaming of going back to your old school or putting on your old uniform. Also, when you see yourself dreaming of climbing a mountain but you end up getting no where, the waster spirit is at work. Seeing yourself being lost in the wilderness is another indication of the waster spirit. It also operates by pressing people down while they are asleep. The spirit of the waster oppresses, suppresses and depresses its victims.

The operations of the waster's spirit is also manifested when you see yourself being violently and sexually abused by a personality while dreaming, if you dream seeing yourself naked or surrounded by feaces, you have to bind the powers of the wasters in your life. If you see yourself crying in the dream until you wake up in real life, you must not fold your hands. If you also see your hair being cut off, or you are pursued by gun men or you find yourself constantly eating or being locked up, all these are the manifestations of the spirit of the waster.

AGENTS OF WASTAGE

1. Sin
2. Household enemies
3. Witchcraft powers
4. Pride
5. Placenta bondage
6. Curses and evil covenants
7. Disobedience to God
8. Familiar spirits
9. Sexual perversion
10. Addiction
11. Unfriendly friends
12. Destructive incantations
13. Powers of the night
14. The destruction at the noon day
15. Spirit wife or husband
16. Laziness
17. Procrastination
18. Planlessness
19. Aimless living

20. Wrong positioning
21. Evil tongue/bad words
22. Evil names

THE WAY OUT

To get rid of the power of the wasters, you must take the following points into cognizance.

1. Quality repentance
2. Complete obedience
3. Violent faith in God
4. Be determined not to be wasted.
5. Wage war against the wasters
6. Barricade your life through the word of God, the wall of fire, the angels of God and the blood of Jesus.

ATTACKED FROM THE DREAM

During one of my overseas ministry trips, I came across an intelligent professor who came to me for prayers. He told me that he had a dream and in that dream, some people came to him with dry pepper in their hands. They said: "Professor, you are about to win a big award. But we will not allow you to win it". They further told him point blank in the dream that they would remove his eyes. Thus, when they remove his eyes, it would be impossible for the professor to win the award. Before the professor could say something, they had poured pepper on him. The dream, he felt pepperish sensations and pains.

In that condition, he suddenly woke up only to discover that he could not see again! Medical doctors examined the eyes in the hospital and could not fathom the cause or the mystery behind his blindness. But, he could no longer see. The powers of the wasters were at work.

*Pray this prayer points with holy anger for good seven times:

1. "I decree and declare to the heavens that my life shall not be wasted".

2. Every powers of my father's house that wants to waste my life, be wasted in the name of Jesus.

CHAPTER TWO

WICKEDNESS MUST DIE

Minister forces, perpetrate wickedness on a daily basis. Tragedy and woe have been the lot of many helpless souls. When you see the marauding powers of darkness, lurking in the dark, to strike a helpless victim, it should send a signal to you that wickedness is at hand.

Many of us today are witnesses to the ever alarming increase in the rate of crime and wickedness which exists in our present milieu. Nowadays, many promising stars have been cut short and many families broken as a result of the terrible manifestations of the forces of darkness.

To aggravate the problem, the African society has provided a platform for wicked powers to perpetrate wickedness. Family altars and household wickedness have not helped matters. Evil foundations are speaking and crying woes to many lives. The activities of witches and wizards are also gaining grounds on a daily basis. Mysterious occurrences are taking place daily. There is wickedness in high places. The high spate of orgy killings in our society, therefore, calls for a quick and calculated step to stem the tide of wickedness.

Against this backdrop, the Church of the living God must not fold hands and watch the powers of darkness perpetrating evil. Power must change hands. The Lord must arise and wipe away the tears of the victims of wickedness. An end must come to the wickedness of the wicked, The enemies of God and the people of God must receive divine chastisement. Enough is enough. You don't have to continue to grope in darkness because the light of God will shine forth and you shall be repositioned and relocated for unprecedented breakthroughs. The time for your deliverance has come.

This is the set time. Your day of deliverance is nearer than you think. God wants to give you the expected deliverance now. Look up! For your salvation draweth near. The enemies of the Lord will be defeated and be confounded. Mountains must bow. Valleys must be rolled away and stumbling blocks must become stepping stones. The Bible says:

Isaiah 42:13-16: *The LORD shall go forth as a mighty man, he shall stir up jealousy like a man of war: he shall cry, yea, roar; he shall prevail against his enemies. I have long time holden my peace; I have been still, and refrained myself: now will I cry like a travailing woman; I will destroy and devour at once. I will make waste mountains and hills, and dry up all their herbs; and I will make the rivers islands, and I will dry up the pools. And I will bring the blind by a way that they knew not; i will lead them in paths that they have not known: I will make darkness light* *before them, and crooked things straight. These things will I do unto them, and not forsake them.*

THE ANOINTING BREAKS THE YOKE

The distinguishing thing that breaks the yoke of wickedness in the life of a man or woman, is the anointing. When the anointing of God comes, stubborn barriers and yokes have no choice than to be broken. It does not matter how many years you have spent under satanic attacks. The wilderness and the bizarre experiences you are going through do not matter. What matters is that, the anointing of God can break every yoke in your life and make you free.

Isaiah 10:27: And it shall come to pass in that day, that his burden shall be taken away from off thy shoulder, and his yoke from off thy neck, and the yoke shall be destroyed because of the anointing.

When God decides to do something, no power on earth or in heaven can say otherwise. God will ever remain God. Nothing whatsoever can erase or defile the rulings of God in the court of heaven. God is ready to put smiles on your face and laughter in your mouth. The wickedness of the wicked has to cease because of divine intervention.

Did I hear you say or think that your case might be Impossible? No! Never! Your case is not beyond redemption. The power of God can do all things no matter your predicament and problems. Just rest under the mighty hands of Jehovah and there will be a mighty shift and relocation from hopeless to hope and from remorse to rejoicing. The Bible attests to the might of the Lord in the Scripture below.

Luke 1:37: for with God nothing shall be impossible.

There is no impossibility in the dictionary of God. If only you can have faith and do your own part of preparing for deliverance, nothing will cut short you hopes and expectation. Have you ever imagined the power that created the whole world failing? I mean, can the power that raised up Lazarus from the dead after three days and caused the red sea to part, ever fail? God will hear your cry. Put your faith in Him and nothing shall be impossible for you.

DIVINE VISITATION BEFORE DELIVERANCE

The operational principle of God is that there is always divine visitation before your deliverance can be determined. When God decides to turn around and fight for you, know that you have been visited by the Lord. Before Abraham and Sarah could have the long standing yoke of barrenness broken, they received divine pronouncement after divine visitation. Do you know that some of the problems which satan puts on your way are blessings in disguise.

Those things are what God will use to catapult you to reaching your divine position. To experience lasting deliverance) you must pray for divine visitation. This, in other words will prepare the ground for your upliftment.

DIVINE INTERVENTION

After divine visitation from the Lord, you will then get divine intervention. Beloved, when you are in a dilemma, you need divine intervention. Also, when all hope is lost, you will cry earnestly for divine intervention.

Have you tried all options and nothing is forthcoming? Then, you need divine intervention which will bring about your expected deliverance. Divine intervention is what you need, when you have tried all possible means and nothing seems to be working for you. Don't be dejected! Look up to your heavenly Father. Tell Him all your fears. Pray violently and there shall be divine intervention on your way.

What then is divine intervention? This is the miracle that will happen to you when you have lost hope. Divine intervention comes on your way when you receive a divine surprise. Divine intervention is the finger or hand of God in the affairs of men.

The kind of miracle that happens to you and will bring tears of joy on your way is what is known as divine intervention. One thing you should know about divine intervention is that, it is the miracle that will happen to you when all hope is lost.

At this point I want you to take the following prayer points with fervent zeal:

1. My Father, look at my situation and visit me in the name of Jesus.

2. Where is the God of Elijah? Arise and manifest your power in my life in the name of Jesus.

3. Every power that wants to waste my life, die in the name of Jesus.

4. Every arrow of witchcraft fired against me, die in the name of Jesus.

5. Oh God arise, and scatter my stubborn pursuers in the name of Jesus.

6. I command my life, to move forward by fire in the name of Jesus.

7. Every owner of evil load in my life, carry your

load by fire in the name of Jesus.

8. Star of my destiny, arise and shine in the name of Jesus.

A VICTOR OR VICTIM

The age in which we live in, is saturated with wickedness, in the most terrible form. As the world becomes a global village with advancements in science and technology, the powers of darkness are also perfecting different strategies for moving to the next level. Spiritual wickedness in high places, are becoming more and more wicked in their operations because they, know that they have but a short time. As a result, multitudes are being wasted daily. What we now have is a mad rush to hell, where sinners will languish through out eternity. If you truly have the mind of Christ, you must arise and do something before you become enlisted among the victims of satanic arrows.

The Bible has not put us in ignorance as to the malevolent forces which occupy different cadres in the satanic kingdom. We are made to understand this fact in the verse below.

Eph 6:12: *For we wrestle not against flesh and blood, but against principalities, against powers, against the rulers of the darkness of this world, against spiritual wickedness in high places.*

THE EVIL AGENDA

Part of the agenda of the last days is that the cohorts and hosts of hell are all out to waste many lives and send them to hell. Prominent among the signs of the last days, is the deterioration of agents of darkness. In other words, they will grow worse in their desire and operations of wickedness.

2 Timothy 3:13: But evil men and seducers shall wax worse and worse, deceiving, and being deceived.

As far as the plan, and purpose of the devil is concerned, you are supposed to fall a victim of the wicked arrows that fly in the day and in the night. But, the will and plan of God for you, is to move from strength to strength and from victory to victory through the fire of our Lord Jesus. A child of God must not be moved by satanic threats.

WICKEDNESS DELINEATED

What then is wickedness? Simply put, wickedness is anything that is evil. To be wicked is to be morally bad. A person who is wicked, will be evil in principles and actions. Also wickedness means to engage in mischief, without any regard for the consequences. To commit wickedness is to commit atrocities and to be fierce, malicious, dangerous, devilish, animalistic, uncultured, unruly, hazardous

WASTING THE WASTERS

and bestial.

When you are wicked, you will be disgustingly unpleasant. Wickedness is to cause harm or distress or trouble. That is why the Bible says that the whole world lies in wickedness. It is crystal clear that all the signs of the last days as predicted by our Lord and Saviour Jesus Christ are fast coming to pass. But one of the neglected signs of the last days is that, there will be satanic revival, which will lead to high increase of calamities, woes and wickedness.

Since the devil and his cohorts know that they have but a short time, they will come out in their thousands to launch a final attack on humanity. The final attack will be desperate, dangerous and highly destructive.
That is why the Bible says

***Revelation 12:12:** Therefore rejoice, ye heavens, and ye that dwell in them. Woe to the inhabiters of the earth and of the sea! for the devil is come down unto you, having great wrath, because he knoweth that he hath but a short time.*

The electronic and print media bear eloquent testimony to the high spate of wickedness in our age, it is no more fantasy to read of heart rendering accounts of ritual killings, murder, suicide, patricide, homicide and other terrific sights that happen in our generation. All these practices are not only restricted to the larger society but they likewise happen even in primary schools, secondary schools and to crown it all our ivory towers. The ivory towers have become the dens of thieves and robbers as many frustrated students are considering robbery as a better option. Now and then, the academic calendars of many higher institutions are dotted by different crimes like rape, occult practices, and fighting. All these despicable acts, plead the schools and the nation at large backward.

It is therefore the responsibility of Christians and the Church of God, to act fast, before the world collapses. Something has to be done. We have the master key of prayers that can unlock any door and even soften any hardened heart.

WICKEDNESS CONDEMNED

God frowns at wickedness of all forms and in any category. Anyone who is wicked will receive the judgment and indignation of God. Let it be settled in your mind that wickedness is sin and anyone who is wicked is a sinner. Wickedness of all sorts and categories will, therefore, attract the wrath of God. The Bible says;

Job 18:5: Yea, the light of the wicked shall be put out, and the spark of his fire shall not shine.

The anger of God, is unleashed on the wicked, on a daily basis. That is why you must detest all manners and forms of wickedness because it might be detrimental to your soul. The Bible makes us to understand this in the book of Psalms

Psalm 7:11: *God judgeth the righteous, and God is angry with the wicked every day.*

Psalm 11:6: *Upon the wicked he shall rain snares, fire and brimstone, and an horrible tempest: this shall be the portion of their cup.*

Anyone who continues in wickedness without repentance will be duly punished by the Lord. Premature death among many other things is the consequence of remaining obstinate in wickedness.

Proverb 2:22: *But the wicked shall be cut off from the earth, and the transgressors shall be rooted out of it.*

Proverb 10:27: *The fear of the LORD prolongeth days: but the years of the wicked shall be shortened.*

Proverb 13:9: *The light of the righteous rejoiceth: but the lamp of the wicked shall be put out.*

The Scripture pronounces woe to the wicked and I believe that any wickedness targeted against you shall be destroyed by the Lord.

Isaiah 3:11: *Woe unto the wicked! It shall be ill with him: for the reward of his hands shall be given him.*

DELIVERANCE PRAYERS MISCONSTRUED

I want to seize this opportunity to clear the air about our deliverance prayers. Quite many people, misconstrue our prayer points. Let me make it categorically clear that, we do not pray against human beings or make them to die. We, however, pray that powers should be destroyed. When we say that a particular power should die, we are otherwise praying that such power should stop its evil activities.

One thing that you should know about human language is that it has the capacity to mean different things. For instance, in English Language, death could signify or mean many things. Death does not only mean to stop living. When something expires, you can say that it is dead. Also, if something stops working or even disappears you can say that it is dead. Apart from that, when you eradicate something, you can say it is dead. That is why you can say that cultism is dead in the family of a person or in the life of a particular person.

Therefore, from the foregoing, we can conclude that death does not just mean to stop breathing. It could as well mean to stop or cease functioning. The literal meaning of death can be seen in the book of Genesis, when God told Adam that the day he tastes the forbidden fruit he would die. Adam took the fruit and still lived longer for about 93 years, the death that God was talking about is figurative (has another meaning). It does not mean that Adam would fall down and stop breathing. The Bible makes it clear to us, that anyone who gives himself or herself to pleasure is dead while he or she is still breathing or alive.

Another point that I want to make clear to you is that, spirits can not die. However, it is possible to stop a particular evil spirit from carrying out evil and demonic activities. Therefore, if you are told to command wickedness to die, it means that you should pray that the power working wickedness against you should stop functioning

THE PRINCIPLES OF OVERCOMING WICKEDNESS

There are certain laid down blueprints that you must bear in mind before you can have the guts to overcome wickedness. Ignorance of these principles might elongate your suffering or even keep you under satanic wickedness and its oppressions.

The first principle is that, before you can have victory over wickedness, there must not be any wickedness in you. No filthiness, wickedness of any sort and manner must be in you. You must be holy, blameless and without wrinkle or blemish. Before you can cripple the activities of a witch, the wickedness in you must be taken out.

The second principle you should know is that wickedness begins, from hell fire and enters into the heart before going into the imagination. From the imagination, it becomes a thought after which it comes into reality. Therefore, you must guard your heart diligently.

The third principle you should understand is that wickedness does not need to have any motive. Therefore, don't keep shouting and crying that you have not done anything wrong. You don't have to do anything wrong before wickedness will come to you.

The fourth principle that must be clear to you is that, there is a serpent and a scorpion behind wickedness. That is why, Jesus gave his disciples power and authority over all the wickedness of serpentine and scorpion spirits.

Mark 16:18: *They shall take up serpents; and if they drink any deadly thing, it shall not hurt them; they shall lay hands on the sick, and they shall recover.*

The fifth principle you need to know is that there is a class of dark powers that specialises in wickedness. The book of Ephesians attests to this fact.

WASTING THE WASTERS 35

Eph. 6:12: *For we wrestle not against flesh and blood, but against principalities, against powers, against the rulers of the darkness of this world, against spiritual wickedness in high places.*

Another principle you must understand is that wickedness is alien to mercy and pity. Wicked powers are not interested in your cries. The only language that they understand is violence.

Also, there are different levels of wickedness. This is obvious. Anyone who steals your bed is a wicked person. But, anyone who steals your sleep is more wicked. Somebody who steals your book is wicked, but anyone who steals your brain is more wicked. There is what is called environmental wickedness, spiritual wickedness, marital wickedness, household wickedness and even career wickedness. You must deal with all these.

CHAPTER THREE

BURIED BUT NOT DEAD

WASTING THE WASTERS

The story of how Lazarus was raised from the dead, is crucial to the understanding of the topic under consideration.

John 11:1-5: *Now a certain man was sick, named Lazarus, of Bethany, the town of Mary and her sister Martha. (It was that Mary which anointed the Lord with ointment, and wiped his feet with her hair, whose brother Lazarus was sick Therefore his sisters sent unto him, saying, Lord, behold, he whom thou lovest is sick. When Jesus heard that, he said, this sickness is not unto death, but for the glory of God, that the Son of God might be glorified thereby. Now Jesus loved Martha, and her sister, and Lazarus.*

Lazarus was described as a person whom the Lord loves. He was a friend of Jesus. Although he was a friend, yet he was sick. The question is "Why was he sick if he was a friend of Jesus". You may put this question in another way, "Can he whom Jesus loves be sick?."

The whole of the family of Mary, Martha and Lazarus were friends of Jesus. In spite of this, tragedy struck. The death of Lazarus was a sad event.

THE PRESENCE OF THE LORD DOES NOT MEAN THE ABSENCE OF DANGER

The first lesson that is very clear and glaring from this passage is that, the presence of the Lord does not excuse you from the problems of life. The fact that you are a Christian does not give you an automatic certificate to be exempted from the battles of life.

The storm of life is likened to a strange personality. It has no respect for academic levels. It has no respect for your family background. Neither does he respect beauty intelligence.

The storms of life are like a stark illiterate. It can not read, neither can it write. It bombards people any how and anywhere. Lazarus was a friend of Jesus, yet, he was sick. You may love the Lord with all your heart and yet you are facing battles. This is not new. It has happened to someone whom Jesus loved- Lazarus by name.

I SHALL RISE AGAIN

When problems arise, some people break down completely. Some go through similar problems and break existing records. The problem could make you better or bitter. I want you to make this declaration now; "I shall not surrender, I shall not give up, my problem shall give up in the name of Jesus"

The Bible says that a righteous man falleth seven times and rise up again. According to Proverbs 24:16.

Proverbs 24:16*: For a just man falleth seven times, and riseth up again: but the wicked shall fall into mischief.*

Falling down is not a symbol of defeat, staying down is the sign of defeat.

PHYSICAL AND SPIRITUAL SICKNESS

There is another lesson to be learnt in this passage.

John 11:4: *When Jesus heard that, he said, this sickness is not unto death, but for the glory of God, that the Son of God might be glorified thereby.*

Jesus said, "This sickness is not unto death" What Jesus said implies that there are some sicknesses that are unto death. Physical and spiritual sickness should not be ignored. Your pride may be a sickness. Your anger may be a sickness. The mild headache or stomach upset which you ignore is a sickness. Unforgiving spirit is a sickness. The bitterness within you is a sickness-a spiritual sickness. If you ignore it, it might develop into serious trouble later. A mild physical or spiritual sickness can lead to death. Immediately Jesus declared, "This sickness is not unto death" His powerful words have melted away the power of sickness.

At this juncture, raise your hand and say, "Lord Jesus, speak death to my sickness in the name of Jesus".

THE POWER OF THE SPOKEN WORD

When Jesus speaks to your circumstances, it may still be visible but it has lost its power. Has the enemy cast you into the furnace of fire'? I assure you that there shall be a "Fourth man" in the fire in the person of the Lord Jesus.

When all things are against you, that is the time when faith prospers. At such a time, your worst can become your best.

At a particular time in the ministry of our Lord Jesus, he came across a fig tree. He was expecting fruit from it but found none. Jesus spoke against the fig tree. The fig tree pretended as if it did not hear the word of Jesus. To the disciples, they felt that nothing really happened. But before the next day the fig tree had obeyed the words of Jesus and dried up.

When your problem hears the word of Jesus today, it will dry up from the root in the name of Jesus. Let Jesus speak to that problem which you have, and it will disappear in the name of Jesus.

NO PANIC

Again, there is a vital lesson which we ought to learn from this single passage.

***John 11:5-7:** Now Jesus loved Martha, and her sister, and Lazarus. When he had heard therefore that he was sick, he abode two days still in the same place where he was. Then after that saith he to his disciples, Let us go into Judaea again.*

Yes, Lazarus was dead. Jesus was called upon to save the situation. The Lord was so mindful of his schedule. He did not abandon what He was doing. He did not act under sentiments. He was not panicky about the situation of Lazarus. Jesus gave death and satan extra days to perform their worst on Lazarus. Jesus Christ is the master of situation and circumstances. He can utter a word and in a moment it would come to pass. When he speaks, he dismantles the castle of the enemy, which he had built for years. Jesus arrived there when all hopes were lost.

A paralysed brother was brought to a Christian meeting. I can remember, clearly, the prayer point that we were praying that fateful morning. The prayer point is, "Anything God has not planted in my life, let it be uprooted". The prayer started and all of a sudden the brother noticed that something was growing out of his head like a horn. The brother held on to the perceived horn on his head and began to pulled it as prayer was still going on. By the time prayer ended he had already pull out a structure which was as long as a ruler out of his body, it is amazing that such a kind of structure could be in the human body.

The brother had been in that paralysed condition for fourteen years. But, a moment of fervent prayer, was enough for him to pull out what the enemy planted in his body for about fourteen years. Jesus arrived when all hopes were completely lost. I believe, too, that you might be in one hopeless condition or the other. You might be thinking that the Lord has forgotten you. In a time like this, when you are at your wit's end then the Lord shall arise on your behalf.

That miracle, which your life demands, shall surely be given unto you in the name of Jesus. Do not lose hope. The Lord is on the throne. Your condition could not be worse than that of Lazarus. If Lazarus could be raised again, my friend do not panic, your miracle is at hand.

Men might look at you and say that you are hopeless but very soon they will realise that your God will never come late. They shall find out that, no condition is hopeless before God. Lift your hands unto heaven and declare this: "I am ripe for a miracle by the power in the blood of Jesus"

IN A MOMENT

In one, day Jesus cancelled the works of satan. With His few words He brought the ugly works of satan, death and hell to nothing.

What has taken the friends so many days or years to accomplish, was dismantled in a moment. What a great God we serve! It does not matter how old your problem is. It does not matter the number of years it has stayed in your body. How long you are caged inside the den of lion is not the most important thing. The important thing is, "Let God arise" and his enemy shall scatter.

Are you struggling against an ancient gate? Are you troubled by an age-long infirmity? The Lord Almighty will arise and deliver you today in Jesus name.

I remember the case of a brother, who was born in a strange village in Nigeria. Strange things take place in the village. Whenever a child was born there, it was a strange voice that would usually dictate what the name of the baby would be. And that is the name the child must bear.

Since the brother happened to come from the same village, he fell victim of the strange occurrence.

The name he bore was the name given by a strange voice. As the name was, so was his life. The translation of the name of the brother is "light feather".

It was observed that the maximum period the brother spent in any place of work he got, was one month before he got sacked. In some places, he would be asked to go home while his termination letter was being typed. Later, the brother took up some aggressive warfare prayers. Through the prayer points, the ancient gates were broken.

The ancient gates of your life shall be broken by the spoken words of the Lord. It does not matter for how many years generational sickness has enveloped you; it will take the master just a moment to rectify the ancient ruins. The words of the Master will wipe away tears and restore joy.

Raise your hands unto heaven and pray thus: "Oh God arise and speak words of breakthroughs into my life in the name of Jesus".

Let us read further

John 11:17-22: Then when Jesus came, he found that he had lain in the grave four days already. Now Bethany was nigh unto Jerusalem, about fifteen furlongs off: And many of the Jews came to Martha and Mary, to comfort them concerning their brother.

Then Martha, as soon as she heard that Jesus was coming, went and met him: but Mary sat still in the house. Then said Martha unto Jesus, Lord, if thou hadst been here, my brother had not died. But I know, that even now, whatsoever thou wilt ask of God, God will give it thee

Martha said, "But I know, that even now". The phrase... "Even now" shows the faith of Martha. Martha was saying, although he was dead, the presence of Jesus could raise Lazarus.

WHEN JESUS COMES

The response of Jesus to the faith of Martha is ... "Thy brother shall rise again" v23

Let us examine verse 28

John 11:28: And when she had so said, she went her way, and called Mary her sister secretly, saying, The Master is come, and calleth for thee.

When Jesus appeared on the scene of an embarrassing storm, he turned a great storm to a great calm. When Jesus arrives he will turn great storm to peace. He will turn your tears to laughter. He will turn sorrow into joy. He wiil turn weeping into laughter. He will turn adversities to triumph. He will turn the night to day. He will turn every frustration to fulfillment. He will turn ashes to beauty. He will turn failure into success.

When Jesus is invited into the scene he will turn poverty into prosperity. He will turn all the destruction to glorious constructions. He will turn disgrace to grace. He will turn weakness to strength. When Jesus comes into the scene, darkness will turn to light and all loss to gain.

Raise your right hand into the heavens again and declare, "My problem, hear the word of the Lord, the Master has come in the name of Jesus"

"Mr. Fear, hear the word of the Lord, the Master has come in the name of Jesus"

"My trouble, you are in trouble today because the Master has come in the name of Jesus".

LOOSE HIM AND LET HIM GO

Jesus gave a word of command and said, "Lazarus come forth" And it was so. Only God can release a spirit from the grave and send it back to the body.

The second miracle that was needed was for grave clothes to be removed from him. The tokens of death still surrounded him after he arose. Jesus now made another word of command, "Loose him and let him go"

WASTING THE WASTERS

The master has spoken the words of life to many but grave clothes still remain on them. There are people who were baptized in the Holy Ghost. They are washed and purified but yet the grave clothes is not yet removed from them. Although Lazarus was liberated, he was yet not free. He was still bound.

Today, we have many born again believers, who are saved, sanctified and spirit filled but still bound. Sin and evil covenant have bound them. The bondage of darkness and the powers of the night and day have put them under bondage..

When a believer is heaven-bound and he is so determined to get there, the devil will be unruffled. He would say, 'I would not say you should not go to heaven. But as you go take along ancient garments of poverty and put on the shoes of sickness and add the tie of constant malaria" The person would go to heaven but with much bruises on his body.

Jesus said, "Loose him and let him go". This is a word of command from heaven. God was the first person to issue such a command. He issued the word to Pharaoh when he said, "Let my people go". Israel was captivated by Pharaoh. The people of God were in the hands of the wicked king. The king was tossing them like a ball. Then, the word of command came against Pharaoh and his men.

"Let my people go". Raise your hands and make this distinct declaration "Ancient foundation of trouble, loose me and let me go in the name of Jesus".

IS THERE ANYTHING TOO HARD FOR THE LORD?

The Bible is a book that is supposed to answer questions. But sometimes, the Bible itself asks questions but gives no answer. For example the Bible says that if the foundation be destroyed, what can the righteous do? The Bible gave no answer to the question.

The Bible asks a question, "When the Son of man come to the earth will he find faith on earth?" Again, to the question the Bible has no answer.

But there is a question that the Bible gave an answer to in *Genesis 18:14a*. It says *"Is any thing too hard for the Lord?"*. The answer to this question is in *Jeremiah 32:17* which says

Jer. 32:17: *Ah Lord GOD! behold, thou hast made the heaven and the earth by thy great power and stretched out arm, and there is nothing too hard for thee.*

There is no promise too hard for the Lord to

fulfill. There is no prayer, too hard for the Lord to answer. There is no problem, too hard for Him to solve. There is no stubborn situation, too hard for God to resolve. There is no enemy, too hard for God to dismantle.

There is no mountain, too high for God to climb. There is no reproach too hard for God to remove.

AWESOME GOD

God is a spirit. He is the Holy one of Israel. He is the God of Abraham, Isaac and Jacob. He is the God of vision, dream and angelic visitation. If He needs to send an angel to resolve your situation, he will send an angel.

God was the one who covered the land with water in His anger in Noah's day. He was the same one who parted the red sea and made the children of Israel to pass on dry land.

God has sent fire, whirlwind, rain and earthquake from heaven before. God has brought water from the rock. God has made snake from wood. Moses threw down his stick and it became a snake. God made man from the dust. He was the one who buried Koran, Dathan, Abiram, and their company alive.

God was excited when Elijah called the prophet

of Baal to contest at mount Carmel. When Elijah said "Let fire fall". God was the one who sent fire on Elijah's altar. God was the same person who turned river Nile to blood. It was God who ordered Jericho walls to fall. It was God who first made an aeroplane called the chariot of fire to carry Elijah from the earth to heaven.

God made three men, to walk through a fiery furnace. He created eyes for a man without eyeball. It was God's angels that dealt with Pharaoh. His angels did terrible warfare in the Bible. Jesus resurrection was announced by angels. When He spoke life to dead matters, they listened to his voice, because He is the resurrection and the life. The grave could not hold Him back on the day of His resurrection.

The voice and the power of resurrection restored Lazarus to life. The grave could not hold Lazarus captive. That is why I am assuring you, that no grave shall limit you henceforth, in the name of Jesus. The Master has come.

Until you meet this awesome God, you are limited. It is high time to pray against grave clothes. It is time to deal with the spirit of limitation. How can somebody who is born again, spirit filled and full of God's power go about with grave clothes in his life?

It is time to call down fire and destroy every limitation. If God needs to demote your enemies let him do so. If He needs to transfer your adversaries let Him do so. If he has to kill let Him kill. If anything would be for the fulfillment of God's purpose for your life, He will do it. The most important thing is that the grave clothes must be removed because the Master is around.

PRAYER POINTS

1. Every grave clothes of my father's house, limiting my life, die, in the name of Jesus.

2. Every power of limitation and disgrace, what are you waiting for? die in name of Jesus.

3. Every power, that wants to bury me while I am alive, die, in the name of Jesus.

4. Oh God arise, and manifest your power as a man of war in my situation in the name.

5. Inherited badluck, die, in the name of Jesus.

6. Every power, that says I will not be congratulated, be wasted in the name of Jesus.

7. My enemy shall die, in my place, in the name of Jesus.

OTHER PUBLICATIONS BY DR. D. K. OLUKOYA

1. Be Prepared
2. Breakthrough Prayers For Business Professionals
3. Brokenness
4. Born Great, But Tied Down
5. Can God Trust You?
6. Criminals in The House Of God
7. Contending For The Kingdom
8. Dealing With Local Satanic Technology
9. Dealing With Witchcraft Barbers
10. Dealing With Hidden Curses
11. Dealing With The Evil Powers Of Your Father's House
12. Dealing With Unprofitable Roots
13. Deliverance: God's Medicine Bottle
14. Deliverance By Fire
15. Deliverance From Spirit Husband And Spirit Wife
16. Deliverance Of The Conscience
17. Deliverance Of The Head
18. Destiny Clinic
19. Drawers Of Power From The Heavenlies
20. Dominion Prosperity
21. Evil Appetite
22. Facing Both Ways
23. Fasting And Prayer
24. Failure in The School Of Prayer
25. For We Wrestle ...
26. Holy Cry
27. Holy Fever
28. How To Obtain Personal Deliverance (Second Edition)
29. How To Pray When Surrounded By The Enemies
30. Idols Of The Heart
31. Is This What They Died For?
32. Limiting God

OTHER PUBLICATIONS BY DR. D. K. OLUKOYA

33. Meat For Champions
34. Overpowering Witchcraft
35. Personal Spiritual Check-Up
36. Power Against Coffin Spirits
37. Power Against Destiny Quenchers
38. Power Against Dream Criminals
39. Power Against Local Wickedness
40. Power Against Marine Spirits
41. Power Against Spiritual Terrorists
42. Power Must Change Hands
43. Pray Your Way To Breakthroughs (Third Edition)
44. Prayer Rain
45. Prayer Strategies For Spinsters And Bachelors
46. Prayers To Move From Minimum To Maximum
47. Prayer Warfare Against 70 Mad Spirits
48. Prayers To Destroy Diseases And Infirmities
49. Praying Against The Spirit Of The Valley
50. Praying To Dismantle Witchcraft
51. Release From Destructive Covenants
52. Revoking Evil Decrees
53. Satanic Diversion Of The Black Race
54. Silencing The Birds Of Darkness
55. Smite The Enemy And He Will Flee
56. Spiritual Warfare And The Home
57. Strategic Praying
58. Strategy Of Warfare Praying
59. Students in The School Of Fear
60. The Enemy Has Done This
61. The Evil Cry Of Your Family Idol
62. The Fire Of Revival
63. The Great Deliverance
64. The internal Stumbling Block

OTHER PUBLICATIONS BY DR. D. K. OLUKOYA

65. The Lord is A Man Of War
66. The Prayer Eagle
67. The Pursuit Of Success
68. The Seasons Of Life
69. The Star in Your Sky
70. The Secrets Of Greatness
71. The Serpentine Enemies
72. The Slow Learners
73. The Snake in The Power House
74. The Spirit Of The Crab
75. The Tongue Trap
76. The Way Of Divine Encounter
77. The Wealth Transfer Agenda
78. The Vagabond Spirit
79. Unprofitable Foundations
80. Victory Over Satanic Dreams (Second Edition)
81. Violent Prayers Against Stubborn Situations
82. War At The Edge Of Breakthroughs
83. When God is Silent
84. Wealth Must Change Hands
85. When You Are Knocked Down
86. Woman! Thou Art Loosed.
87. Your Battle And Your Strategy
88. Your Foundation And Destiny
89. Your Mouth And Your Deliverance
90. Adura Agbayori (Yoruba Version Of The Second Edition Of Pray Your Way To Breakthroughs)
91. Awon Adura Ti Nsi Oke Nidi (Yoruba Prayer Book)
92. Pluie De Prières
93. Esprit Vagabondage
94. En Finir Avec Les Forces Maléfiques De La Maison De Ton Père

OTHER PUBLICATIONS BY DR. D. K. OLUKOYA

95. Que l'envoutement périsse
96. Frappez l'adversaire Et il Fuira
97. Comment Recevoir La Délivrance Du Mari Et De La Femme De Nuit
98. Comment Se delvrer Soi-même
99. Pouvoir Centre Les Terroristes Spiritueis
100. Prières De Percées Pour Les Hommes D'affaires
101. Prier Jusqu'a Remporter La Victoire
102. Prières Violentes Pour Humilier Les Opiniâtres
103. Le Combat Spirituel Et Le Foyer
104. Bilan Spirituel Personnel
105. Victoire Sur Les Rêves Sataniques
106. Prayers That Bring Miracles
107. Let God Answer By Fire
108. Prayers To Mount With Wings As Eagles
109. Prayers That Bring Explosive increase
110. Prayers For Open Heavens
111. Prayer To Make You Fulfill Your Divine Destiny
112. Prayers That Make God To Answer And Fight By Fire
113. Prayers That Bring Unchallengeable Victory And Breakthrough Rainfall Bombardments.
114. The Mysteries Of Life

BOOK ORDER

Is there any book written by **Dr. D. K. Olukoya**
(General Overseer MFM Ministries) that you would like to have:

Have you seen his latest books?
To place order for this End-Time materials,
Text your request as follows

- Book title(s)
- Delivery Address

Call: 08161229775

Battle cry ministries ... equipping the saint of God
God bless

www.ingramcontent.com/pod-product-compliance
Lightning Source LLC
LaVergne TN
LVHW051203080426
835508LV00021B/2782